Autism

ANN O. SQUIRE

Children's Press®
An Imprint of Scholastic Inc.

Content Consultant
Karen E. Peters, DrPH
Clinical Assistant Professor
Division of Community Health Sciences
University of Illinois–Chicago, School of Public Health
Chicago, Illinois

Library of Congress Cataloging-in-Publication Data
Squire, Ann O.
 Autism / by Ann O. Squire.
    pages cm. — (A true book)
 Includes bibliographical references and index.
 ISBN 978-0-531-21473-2 (library binding) — ISBN 978-0-531-21523-4 (pbk.)
1. Autism—Juvenile literature. 2. Autism in children—Juvenile literature. I. Title.
 RC553.A88S68 2016
 616.85'882—dc23   2015003912

© 2016 Scholastic Inc.
All rights reserved. Published in 2016 by Children's Press, an imprint of Scholastic Inc.
Printed in China 62
SCHOLASTIC, CHILDREN'S PRESS, A TRUE BOOK™, and associated logos are trademarks and/or registered trademarks of Scholastic Inc.
1 2 3 4 5 6 7 8 9 10 R 25 24 23 22 21 20 19 18 17 16

Front cover: A boy playing with a large jigsaw puzzle

Back cover: A silhouette of a child's head with puzzle pieces representing autism

Find the Truth!

Everything you are about to read is true *except* for one of the sentences on this page.

Which one is **TRUE**?

T or F   Children with autism often avoid making eye contact.

T or F   A quick blood test can show whether a person has autism.

Find the answers in this book.

Contents

THE BIG TRUTH!

The Genetics of Autism

**Many more boys than girls
are diagnosed with autism.**

The sights, sounds, and smells that surround us can be overwhelming to someone with autism.

Heredity is one factor that contributes to autism.

What Can It Be?

As soon as the after-school bell rang, Claire gathered up her books. She quickly headed outside to wait for her friend Annie. Claire and Annie walked home together every day. They were both in fourth grade and had been best friends since kindergarten. They both loved playing soccer, eating ice cream, and walking their dogs. They also both had baby brothers who were two years old.

⬅ If your sibling has autism, it can help to share your feelings with others.

Tommy and Danny

As they walked, Annie talked about her brother, Tommy. He was starting to put words together to ask for things. "More milk!" and "Doggy go out!" were his favorite phrases. He also noticed

everything around him, pointing to airplanes, cars, and trucks. Even though he was only two years old, Annie had a great time playing with him. He had favorite books and loved to point out the pictures as Annie read the words.

Most toddlers point to images and objects to show interest in them.

Most babies love to interact with others through games like peekaboo.

Claire didn't know what to say. Her brother, Danny, was nothing like Tommy. Danny rarely smiled. He wasn't interested in playing peekaboo or looking at things Claire tried to show him. In fact, Danny didn't notice people or things much at all. Also, while Tommy was starting to run and climb, Danny was hardly walking. He could say a few words, but he wasn't really communicating. It seemed as if Danny was living in his own world.

People on the autism spectrum may fixate on spinning objects, such as fans, clothes in a washing machine, or toys they spin themselves.

Making a Diagnosis

Babies learn and grow at different rates. For a while, Claire's parents thought Danny was just taking a little longer than other babies to start babbling, talking, and walking. But the family soon became worried that Danny didn't pay attention to sounds, people, and objects around him. They wondered if he might have hearing problems. Claire's parents scheduled an appointment with the **pediatrician** to find out more.

 Unusual or repetitive behaviors are common among people with autism.

Seeing the Doctor

The doctor agreed that Danny's **development** was not as fast as expected. A test revealed that the boy's hearing was fine. Deafness was not the problem.

The doctor thought Danny might have an autism **spectrum** disorder (ASD). This affects a person's ability to communicate and interact with other people. The doctor recommended the family visit a developmental pediatrician. These doctors focus on a child's learning abilities and behaviors, such as sitting, talking, and playing with toys. These activities are called developmental milestones.

The developmental pediatrician informed Danny's parents that there is no simple test, such as a blood test, for ASD. There are also no clear physical signs that a child has the disorder. To reach a **diagnosis**, the doctor needed to talk with the parents. She'd learn what Danny could and couldn't do, and how he acted at home. She would compare Danny's development to what children typically learn by certain ages. Finally, she would observe Danny's behavior herself.

Doctors look for clues in a child's abilities and behavior to diagnose an ASD.

13

Talking to the Parents

The doctor reviewed Danny's past health. She asked about his behavior as an infant. Had he always been slow to develop? Or had he stopped doing things he had once been able to do? Gaining and then losing abilities such as speech or making eye contact may be a sign of autism. Did Claire have developmental or learning problems? Having a relative with autism or with attention or learning problems such as Attention Deficit Disorder (ADD) increases the chances of developing autism.

Doctors need to know as much as they can about a patient's past and current health to make an accurate diagnosis.

14

Tablet computers may help autistic children learn and communicate, whether their symptoms are mild or severe.

Next, Danny's parents filled out a checklist that focused on the boy's language, movement, and social skills. The doctor explained that autism is a group of disorders in several areas. The symptoms range from mild to severe. This is why autism is called a spectrum disorder. ASD symptoms fall on a spectrum, or range, of severity. The parents' answers on the checklist would show how serious Danny's disorder might be. They would also highlight the areas where he had the most trouble.

Many people with ASD are very sensitive to sound. Headphones can be helpful in these cases by screening out a lot of the noise.

Autism affects a person's ability to communicate and interact with others. To reach a diagnosis, a doctor would want to watch how a patient behaves in various situations. The doctor had Danny take part in an hour-long assessment, during which Danny performed different tasks. The activities focused on four areas: play, imagination, communication, and social interaction. Problems in any of the areas might indicate autism.

Connecting on the Spectrum

Interacting with others can be challenging for someone with autism. Here are some ways you can help make it easier.

- *Be aware of the environment.* Are there a lot of noises, lights, or other distractions? You may need to find a quieter place.
- *Be direct.* Processing language may be challenging for someone with autism. Use short, simple sentences.
- *Be patient.* He or she might need time to process what you say.
- *Ask before touching the person.* An unexpected touch can be startling. Also, some people are not comfortable with physical contact.
- *Be kind.* Everyone experiences the world differently. Behaviors that seem unusual may just be ways to stay calm or express an emotion or idea.

Some kids with autism find the movement of a swing calming.

18

What Is Autism?

The autism spectrum covers a range of disorders related to development of the brain and **nervous system** during infancy and early childhood. People with autism have difficulties in three areas: communication, relationships, and behavior.

However, individuals with autism have strengths, too. You may meet someone on the spectrum with an amazing memory or a talent for drawing. Someone else may be great at reading maps or excellent at math.

Communication and Relationships

Communication problems affect the ability to form relationships with others. People with autism may find it difficult to use words, facial expressions, gestures, or touch (such as hugs). They may have a hard time figuring out how others are feeling and can have trouble expressing their own emotions. People with severe autism may not be able to use words to communicate at all.

Special teachers work with people who have autism to help them improve their communication skills.

Repetitive movements such as rocking, pacing, hand-flapping, tapping the ears, or snapping fingers are very common among people with ASD.

Behaviors

Children with autism often show unusual behaviors. They might rock back and forth, pace up and down, and even bite or harm themselves. They might be withdrawn and avoid eye contact, not noticing people or things in their environment. Some people with autism are very sensitive to certain sounds or smells, to touch, or to other stimulation. Some may also develop **epilepsy**. This is a brain disorder that causes seizures.

The Spectrum

Some people are diagnosed with classic autistic disorder. This happens when he or she has problems in all three areas (communication, relationships, and behavior). Many people with this diagnosis fall on the more disabled end of the spectrum. People who have severe autism may need help taking care of themselves throughout their lives.

Another type of ASD has the confusing name PDD-NOS. This stands for pervasive developmental disorder–not otherwise specified. People with PDD-NOS usually have problems in one or two areas, but not all three. The symptoms of PDD may be very mild. However, some cases may be more serious.

Autism Spectrum Disorder

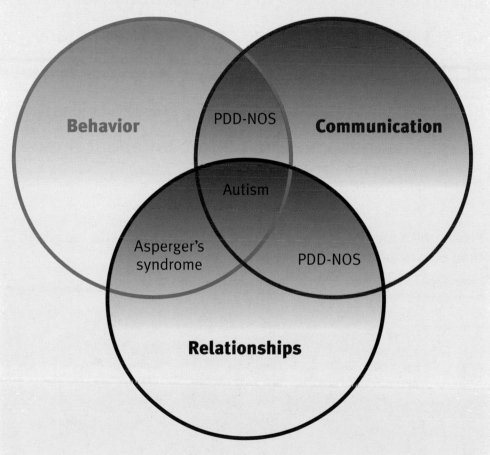

This diagram shows the three areas of difficulty for people on the autism spectrum and how they may overlap. People on the spectrum may have mild, moderate, or severe deficits or challenges in any—or all—of the areas.

One milder form of autism is called Asperger's syndrome. People with Asperger's tend to be very intelligent with above-average vocabularies. They do not have the language challenges that many on the spectrum do. In fact, they tend to talk a lot about topics that interest them. They may read deeply and become super-informed about their areas of interest.

People with Asperger's tend to have an easier time with language than others on the autism spectrum.

Some families have more than one child with autism. In other families, only one child has the disorder.

What Causes Autism?

Just as autism isn't one single disorder, it doesn't have one single cause. Scientists are not sure exactly why ASD develops in one person and not another. Studies have shown that autism tends to run in families. If a parent, brother, or sister has autism, it increases a person's chances of having it. But heredity isn't the whole story. It seems that people inherit a tendency to become autistic, not the disorder itself.

Developing babies receive nutrients and oxygen from their mothers.

Environmental Triggers

Scientists believe that environmental factors may also play a role. For example, they are trying to learn how a mother's health may affect her child's chances of developing autism. They are also studying whether exposure to certain chemicals in the environment during pregnancy may be a contributing factor. Sometimes babies are born weighing too little or much more than average. Other babies are born too soon in the pregnancy. All these factors might make a baby more likely to develop an ASD.

Understanding exactly how heredity and environment influence ASD will take much more study. The research is urgent because autism is on the rise. Scientists have noticed a big increase in the number of ASD diagnoses in recent years. In 2000, roughly 1 in 150 children in the United States were diagnosed with autism. Today, experts estimate that the number is closer to 1 in 68. Further exploration into environmental factors may hold important clues as to why this is happening.

Babies born prematurely are at a much greater risk of developing issues such as autism.

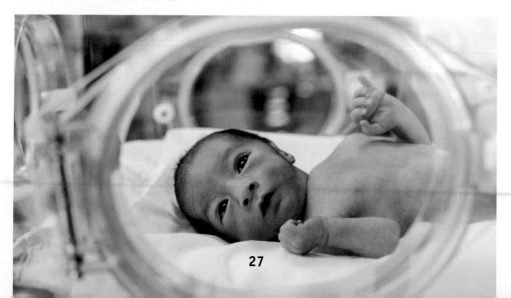

The Genetics of Autism

Inside every cell in your body is a set of instructions that specify many things about you. They determine whether your eyes will be blue or brown, whether you will be left- or right-handed, and so on. These instructions are called genes. They are lined up along structures called chromosomes. Chromosomes are arranged in pairs. One member of each pair came from your mother and the other came from your father.

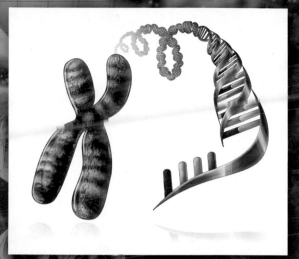

Sometimes, chromosomes and genes change, or mutate. You may have received a mutated gene from a parent. It may also have mutated as your cells divided before you were born. Sometimes a mutation is harmless, affecting a person's eye or hair color, height, or a similar trait. Mutations may also cause problems, such as a birth defect, a disease, or a tendency to develop a disease or disorder.

Scientists believe that irregularities in genes can set the stage for the development of autism. They are currently studying exactly how this happens. Recently, scientists found that hundreds of different genes may be involved. Complex genetic factors may explain why there are so many different types of autism. They may also explain why many more boys than girls develop the disorder.

Special environments called multi-sensory rooms provide safe, comfortable places for people with ASD to play, learn, explore, and relax.

CHAPTER 4

Treating Autism

After a number of tests and assessments, Danny was diagnosed with autistic disorder. The family was relieved to find out what was wrong. At the same time, they were very worried about Danny. Their doctor, however, was hopeful. She said that while autism has no cure, the earlier it is diagnosed and treated, the more progress a patient can make. Danny had just turned two years old. He was at a good age to begin treatment.

 Children with autism tend to be very sensitive to their environments.

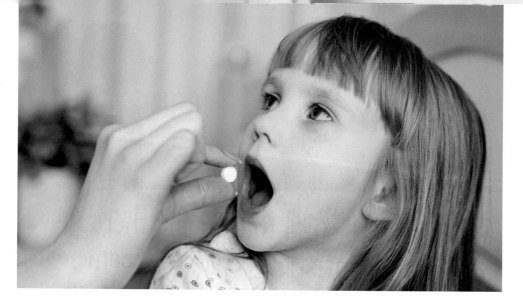

Medications continue to progress and improve as scientists look for new ways to treat autism.

Medications for Autism

Along with undergoing therapy, many people with ASD take medications. These medicines may relieve irritability or help kids pay attention at school. They might also help reduce tantrums, aggression, or repetitive behaviors. When children with autism are calmer, they are better able to learn new skills and desirable behaviors. Scientists are also working to develop medications to help normalize the brain functions involved in autism.

The Vaccine Myth

One fact scientists know for certain is that **vaccines** do not cause ASD. In 1998, a group of researchers claimed to find a link between autism and a common childhood vaccine. However, their study had serious flaws, including falsified (made up) information. The researchers later admitted their claims were inaccurate. In addition, other studies have all proven no connection between the vaccine and ASD.

The idea that a vaccine could cause autism is scary. However, this vaccine and others are not only safe, but also important. They help protect whole communities from dangerous illnesses. Vaccines have even completely wiped out certain diseases, including polio and smallpox, saving countless lives.

Having a Sibling With Autism

If you have a brother or sister who has an ASD, you probably have many different feelings. Having a sibling on the autism spectrum can be tough. You may feel that family life revolves around your brother or sister and his or her challenges. Sometimes it may seem that your parents don't have time for you because they are so busy with your sibling. You might also feel embarrassed when your sibling has tantrums, doesn't speak, or rocks back and forth.

Talking and Learning

You might also be a bit confused about exactly what autism is. At times you may feel jealous of friends with brothers and sisters who are not disabled. All these feelings are normal. If you're feeling sad or confused or left out, talk to your parents. It can also help to talk to other kids who deal with autism. They will understand better than anyone what you are going through. Many communities offer groups where kids meet and share their experiences.

It can help to talk about your experiences with other people in similar situations.

Many children become very close with siblings who have autism.

Despite the challenges, many kids form a special bond with their siblings who are on the spectrum. Because they understand their siblings' challenges, they take pride in their brothers' or sisters' achievements. They also know and appreciate their siblings' strengths better than just about anyone. They may become their siblings' advocates, helping them navigate the world. And they are often their siblings' biggest fans. ★

True Statistics

Number of Americans living with an autism spectrum disorder: 3.5 million

Overall proportion of children in the United States with an ASD: 1 in 68

Proportion of boys versus girls with an ASD: 1 in 42 boys versus 1 in 189 girls

Percent of children with an ASD who eventually develop epilepsy: 20 to 30

Percent of people with autism who also have another genetic disease: 10

Percent of the world's population with an ASD: 1

Percent of people with autism who cannot speak: 25

Did you find the truth?

T Children with autism often avoid making eye contact.

F A quick blood test can show whether a person has autism.

Resources

Books

Elder, Jennifer. *Different Like Me: My Book of Autism Heroes*. London: Jessica Kingsley Publishers, 2006.

Verdick, Elizabeth, and Elizabeth Reeve. *The Survival Guide for Kids with Autism Spectrum Disorders (and their Parents)*. Minneapolis: Free Spirit Publishing, 2012.

Visit this Scholastic Web site for more information on autism:
★ www.factsfornow.scholastic.com
Enter the keyword **Autism**

Important Words

chromosomes (KROH-muh-sohmz) — structures inside a cell that carry the genes that give living things their individual characteristics

development (duh-VEH-lup-muhnt) — a specified state of growth or advancement

diagnosis (dye-uhg-NOH-sis) — identification of what disease a patient has or what the cause of a problem is

epilepsy (EP-uh-lep-see) — a disease of the brain that may cause a person to have sudden blackouts or seizures

nervous system (NUR-vuhs SIS-tuhm) — the system in the body that includes the brain, spinal cord, and nerves

pediatrician (pee-dee-uh-TRI-shuhn) — a doctor who specializes in the care and treatment of babies and children

spectrum (SPEK-truhm) — a wide range

therapy (THER-uh-pee) — a treatment for an injury, disability, or psychological problem

vaccines (vak-SEENZ) — substances used to protect a person from a particular disease

Index

Page numbers in **bold** indicate illustrations.

About the Author

Ann O. Squire is a psychologist and an animal behaviorist. Before becoming a writer, she studied the behavior of rats, tropical fish in the Caribbean, and electric fish from central Africa. Her favorite part of being a writer is the chance to learn as much as she can about all sorts of topics. In addition to *Autism* and books on other health topics, Dr. Squire has written about many different animals, from lemmings to leopards and cicadas to cheetahs. She lives in Long Island City, New York.